WHEN DIVAS DANCE:
THE DIVA SQUAD POETRY COLLECTIVE

Edited by
Chezia Thompson Cager

Maisonneuve Press

© 2004 Chezia Thompson Cager
Photographs by John Shore
The Diva Squad Poetry Collective as a name is a copyright of
Chezia Thompson Cager. All rights reserved.

Published by Maisonneuve Press
P.O. Box 2980
Washington, D.C. 20013
www.maisonneuvepress.com
Telephone: 301.277.7505

Design by Angelo Alcasabas

No part of this publication may be reproduced, or stored in a retrieval system, or transmitted in any form or by any means, electronic, mechanical, photocopying, recording, or otherwise without the written permission of the copyright holder or her estate manager.

To contact the editor, write to the publisher or email to dr.cbt@verizon.net or go to www.spectrumofpoeticfire.com.

Library of Congress Cataloging-in-Publication Data

When divas dance : the Diva Squad Poetry Collective / edited by Chezia Thompson-Cager.
   p. cm.
  ISBN 0-944624-43-X (alk. paper)
1. American poetry--Maryland--Baltimore. 2. American poetry--African American authors. 3. American poetry--Women authors. 4. African American women--Poetry. 5. American poetry--21st century. 6. Baltimore (Md.)--Poetry. I. Thompson-Cager, Chezia.
  PS559.B3W48 2004
  811'.60809287'08996073--dc22

2004006015

ISBN 0-944624-43-X

ACKNOWLEDGEMENTS

Many thanks to the following publications, which published the poems in this volume:

Chezia Thompson Cager
"Malcolm X," *WordWrights*, March-April, 2001
"Strong Women Do Not Want to Keep A Man" and "The Heart is a
    Lonely Hunter: Urse's Song & Bess' Lament" from *Beaded Words: Poems
    Celebrating Joyce J. Scott's exhibit "Kicking It With the Old Masters"
    Performed at The Baltimore Museum of Art*
"Momma's Dancing Shoes' Blues," presented in concert by *The Moving
    Company Dance Theatre*, 2002
"Laura Nyro Dances," *Poetry New Zealand*, Volume 25, 2002
"The First Ho In Space," *Gargoyle Volume 45*, 2002
"Blues For Josephine Baker" in "Sketchbooks" (or Notebooks - I Can't
    Remember): An Artscape 2003 Exhibit/Pinkard Gallery
"The Mayor of Gilmor Street," *Baltimore Review Volume IV
    No. 1*, Winter, 2000
"Wind in the CANE XII" from *Power Objects: A Messge In A Bottle
    For My Daughter and Her Friends – Chapbook-Artscape 1996 – Poetry
    Competition Award*
"Rodin's 'The Thinker' Reflects On Lynching As A National Past Time," *Poet
    Lore Volume 97 Number 3/4*, Fall/Winter, 2002
"The Labyrinth" presented in concert by *The Moving Company Dance
    Theatre*, 2003

Clarinda Harriss
"Downtown Hot September," *Smart Pace*, Spring, 2000
"Local Fauna," *Trouvere*, Spring, 2000
"My Claustrophobic Valentine" *(Best of Issue Award)*, *Poets Domain*, Vol. 25,
    Fall, 1998
"Unasked Question Whose Answer is Love," *Poets Domain*, Vol. 25,
    Fall, 1998
"Hauling the Dog," *Spoon River Anthology*, Spring, 1998
"Crabfingers," *Genre*, 15, 1994
"Mozart Night," Function at the Junction, Spring, 1997
"Thunder," *Timber Creek Review*, March 2001
"Sundial," *The Baltimore Sun*, February, 1995

Kendra Kopelke
"Ode at the End of the Century," *Cream City Review*
"To An Old Sucker Fish," *Agni Review*
"City Rooster," *Maryland Poetry Review*
"Woman in Her Late Thirties," *Maryland Poetry Review*
"To My Thumb," *Function at the Junction*
"Dogs," *Nightsun*
"These Fish," *Black Moon*
"Squirrel-O-Mania," *Dancing Shadow Review*
"Woman With Hamster," *Dancing Shadow Review*
"Carpe Diem, Ants," *The Pearl*
"Eating Out," *Joe*
"Elegy for the Cigarette," *Function at the Junction*

Thanks also to The Seedbed of Irony Press, where these poems first appeared in a limited edition, hand-made letterpress collection entitled *Carpe Diem, Ants*.

The writers would also like to thank the Maryland State Arts Council for grants which made the writing of these poems possible.

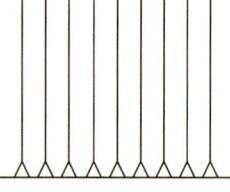

This book is dedicated to the Women and the Men who pushed us forward into our mutual destinies: but especially for Josephine Jacobsen who nurtured us all.

Blessed Be

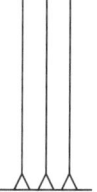

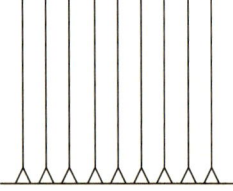

Table Of Contents

Prologue	11
I. Chezia Thompson Cager *"Got To Stir It Up…"*	13
Charm City Charm	14
Night Garden:Fabric Art	15
When Sound Met Matter	16
Evolution: Red Angels	18
The Black Dog of Fate	19
Country Watermelon	23
Malcolm X	24
Tornado Tale/Cuentro De En Tornado	25
The Heart Is A Lonely Hunter: Urse's Song/Bess' Lament	32
Momma's Dancing Shoes Blues	33
Laura Nyro Dances	34
The First Ho In Space/El Primer Ho En El Espacio	35
Blues For Josephine Baker	36
Strong Women Do Not Want To Keep A Man	38
The Mayor of Gilmor Street	40
Wind In the CANE XII	43
Rodin's 'The Thinker' Reflects On Lynching	
As A National Past-time	44
The Labyrinth	45
Cowboy Surgeon	46
Entering Into The Beginning of Myself	47
II. Clarinda Harriss *"I am the Voice…"*	49
Bondo	50
My Claustrophobic Valentine	51
Thunder	52
Babel	53
After the Baby Funeral	54
Crabfingers	55
Spendthrift	56
He Can. She Can	57
Lost Dog Possibilities	58
Hauling the Dog	59
Numina	60

—CLARINDA HARRISS *continued*

Boss Mama's Funeral	61
Pit Bull Owl	62
Local Fauna	65
The Stand-off	66
At Camden Yards	68
Oh: A Footnote on the History of Damita Jo Singer, 1930-1998	69
Summer: Time	70
Weeding	71
Mozart Night: at the Meyerhoff:: Stains on a Long White Dress	72
"Sundial," 410-783-1800	73
Union Memorial Hospital	74
Downtown Hot September	75

III. KENDRA KOPELKE *"She's Got Bette Davis Eyes..."* — 77

Carpe Diem, Ants	78
Box Turtle	80
Annual Exam	81
City Rooster	82
Dogs	84
Eating Out	86
Elegy For The Cigarette	87
Ode At The End Of The Century	89
Squirrel-O-Mania	90
These Fish	93
To My Thumb	95
To An Old Sucker Fish	96
Woman In Her Late Thirties	98
Woman With Hamster	99

THE AUTHORS — 101

Prologue

Myth

Once I believed nothing unintended
passed over my face.
That I was placid-seeming
as a flower, virtuosic
at being seen...

I will tell you I went down
in all earnestness, to the cold,
clear water to see
what I'd made of myself.

There was the way I bent to drink,
there was the terrible grace of my neck.
And though I held very still
in the long gaze of embellishment,
what I saw could not be fixed
by falling in love with it.

LIA PURPURA
From *Stone Sky Lifting*
Ohio State Universuty Press

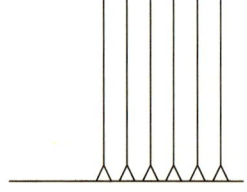

Chezia Thompson Cager

*"Got to stir it up, Got to shake it up Now
When I think about tomorrow..."*

"Stir It Up" sung by Patti LaBelle
On *Patti LaBelle* by MCA Records 1996
Produced by Keith Forsey & Harold Faltermeyer
Originally MCA Records single

Charm City Charm

The Sea Urchin's nest rises
To provide a place for an unsung incantation
As the Seahorse nears the end of his pregnancy
He knows there is no death in spirit
As the Red Moon starts its ascent over the harbor

A call to the Iroquois buried under Mount Royal
A call to the Africans lost in Park Circle
A call to the Irish under Pratt Street
A call to the Polish who created Pigtown
An order to them all to be courageous emotionally

A solstice night to connect dry bones
To lift the mirror of historical envy
Wipe clean the face of annihilation
Restore ragtime health to the dance under this Yellow Moon
It is tiresome being anywhere but in the now moment

Summoned are the hants of the great wharf fire
Summoned are the soldiers delivered dead on the colored trains
Summoned are the iron workers from Turner Station
Summoned are the experimental patients from Johns Hopkins Hospital
Summoned are the children who died working in the clothing industry

And what do we do together
We step into Time and 'Black-Bottom' our way to the truth
We pick up nonchalance and immature and initiate them into maturity
We close the circle midair and declare it unbroken – declare it whole as
The Urchin's nest allows the Seahorse to deliver a celestial wonder
That ascends with the White Moon out of sight

Night Gardens: Fabric Art

dark flowers in black fricative shades
word pictures in mountain peaks
rich burgundies with leftover parts
of the blues that turquoise skies can not
touch in cotton, linen
and hand-woven fabrics
printed rectangular boxes of
ancient exotic visual patterns
Africa, South America, India stand next to
black Muslim tracks bordered by
colored hand-stitching re-defining
the shape and color of the
monsters in the deep that
are not easily seen in our minds

When Sound Met Matter

The 1st Day
At skyrise, Sound came out purple: Circled the Earth 7 times screaming hieroglyphics:
Intersecting with Matter, they did the wild thing.

The 2nd Day
Awaking, Sound went looking for Matter and only found her clothes:
Leaving the crevice, he punched Mars for sneaking a peek while they were cruising.

The 3rd Day
Mars complained to Matter and she realigned the planets
Starting their croon in harmony; bass kicking back on cue.

The 4th Day
Sound stayed up all eon rolling bones on Andromeda with SUN RA
Who warned him about Earth.

The 5th Day
Matter rebelled planting her great webbed feet on Venus' land and Uranus' sea

The 6th Day
Sound set himself on fire and became the Sun's blue black crevice
Sucking up his own caustic rays.

The 7th Day
Matter changed the planets orbital alignments again
Put on new clothes and started radiating a new rhythm in the hum

The 8th Day
Sound reached for her from his cave. To escape him, Matter ascended as a giant electric orb sitting motionless in the sky for a millennium

The 9th Day
Finally touching, they metamorphosized into the single note at the top of the creation ladder – a black star imploding, shifting the universe: Weeping Matter held the note

The 10th Day
The Moon was dancing through elliptical aria runs: Raggedy planets lost their way: The Matrix crashed revealing the Sun hallucinating black angels circling its radiant rim

The 11th Day
Delighted that the Cosmic Ancients were distracted, Disorder appeared and attacked Order in an open bleeding sky: It rained pain until Sound trapped Matter in a Nelson kiss

The 12th Day
Open, Matter struggled with being grounded in the social order of Sound's language: What was might never be again, if Anarchy ruled: Love is the way: The Arguing must end

The 13th Day
Reified, Order reasserted a balanced universe and the shining star of Sound locked in the luminous crescent moon of Matter's embrace, went out for a lover's walk to birth Music.

Evolution: Red Angels
(for choreographer, Richard Dove)

here is where races begin in
the backward lean of a black woman
in a white man's arms
the slide registry sensuality

of an angry violin running with him to
and fro like a pendulum with legs and
arms swiveling hips and shoulders
that shudder and coil and move forward

such a song of straight-legged white romance
apart in cells of light
rejoined in sound as a swift drag
who's in control in whose arms

together they are just leggy harmonies
looking for stability in rhythm's answer
a place of distance separating them
just red angels engulfed in blood light

THE BLACK DOG OF FATE
(because of the *Arkansas Timber Wolf*)

Fred Marks Time in the Wrong Place
    The Dog lounged on the street corner
    watching Fred amusingly shake his head
    at the cow pasture that the Blackfeet had
    passed through in a hurry, leaving Little Rock.
    Notorious for a certain kind of beauty, Fred
    would have to be suicidal to act like he
    appreciated it in 1909.
    The Dog tugged at his meticulously starched
    and ironed shirt-sleeve but he stood there
    trapped between amusement and intense delight,
    as the white woman sauntered across the street
    shaking her ass like a Cocker Spaniel, just for him.

The Brotherhood's idea of Patriotism is a Lynching Party
    "Expect visitors," The Sheriff said tipping his hat to Ida.
    Fred accused of desecrating the flower of white womanhood,
    had to run or stay and die, like a man.
    Ida fought him for their life together: fought him to believe
    he was a man in her eyes, alive – her man: and James was
    the sparkling apple of her eye and the reason they had to go now!
    Too little to endure the fast run, he would have to be left at Auntie's.
    A little food, a bundle of clothes and each other,
    "we have each other," Ida told Fred over and over again.
    The Dog had orders to bring James to St. Louis when he was old enough.
    Reverberating pain, the Dog and the 5 year cried their goodbyes
    and then went silent for months.

The Black Dog From the Blue Lodge Keeps His Watch
    The unpaved rock-strewn road bordering the farm opened up.
    with the Dog's barking.
    James nodded to the Dog, his closest friend on his 13th birthday.
    Dressed in his father's old but clean flannel shirt, dungarees
    with his hunting vest and boots on, he put a book of matches,
    his domino ivories, some more ammunition and the Bible
    that he couldn't really read in a flour sack.
    Daddy's squirrel rifle across his shoulder, he started out with the Dog leading.
    The last thing Fred had done was teach the Dog the Mason signal

that would stop the train.
He put the gold ring with the blue stone he needed to send the signal
around the Dog's neck on a silver chain saying, "Bring my boy to me, ya hear."

The Moon's A Harsh Mistress
Her strawberry hair chased butterflies through the fields,
as she insisted on a game of "Kiss and Tag."
Girls were always disturbing somebody's work!
What was God thinking anyway when he made them?
She knew the rules like he did: just trying to get him killed.
Folks said he was a handsome strapping Thompson.
She was Arkansas pretty but he didn't know what to make of it all.
The dog looked at him saying, "It's time" and he had prepared his goodbyes.
Walking from can't see in the morning to can't see at night:
talking to himself aloud, sounding through new words in the Bible,
hunting in the day, sleeping in tree stars at night,
James felt the happiest he had felt since his parents had fled.

Every Closed Eye Ain't Shut
Running, activated the Dog's "seeing eye."
More apprehensive, he chose a less traveled path.
The freight train would be the last leg of the journey.
Almost there, the Dog dug up eatable roots and spotted berries.
James grilled game over an open fire.
As they were about eat this evening a pale, pretty young
white woman walked out of the brush all dressed up and
asked to warm herself at their fire.
The Dog growled caution but James nodded okay.
And when she had done just that she started away only to turn and say
"I'd be beholding to ya if you would walk aways with me: I'm going
to a big party and you can come too; but you have to stay with the colored."

James Encounters Destiny
An only child, James thought some company - after the weeks on the road -
would be fun and after all, she obviously needed protecting out here alone.
She knelt with up raised arms in her elaborate white gown and pearls,
rubbing the Dog's dirty head saying,
"Ka jooj me Nile. Judge me as water! Shango.

This is a test your ward must pass.
He may win the wealth of Pharaoh or perhaps his most precious dream."
The Dog read her as spirit – no form.
"Afefe Lele nii sewe igi oko laalo.
Gentile breeze is it that bends the leaves of the farm trees.
The Blue Lodge acknowledges your protection Mistress."
They would accompany her.

Time As A Hole In Your Soul Dances
Dustless, sparkling chandeliers illuminated the British china and flatware
choreographed as forms on the imported mahogany table; dwarfed by
the plates of baked duck, roasted deer, fried chicken, cornbread, biscuits
vegetables and desserts. Flutes of wine, mugs of beer, snifters of brandy
and jars of white lightning caught the evening light.
The colored people with their fiddler out back congregated joyously,
with all the same goodies in molded fire clay dishes and baskets.
James got food to tide him over, tips for the trail, advice about the big city,
including how to find his parents- and more clothes than he could carry.
The Dog lay snuggling with a baby girl named Emma,
who helped wash and feed him while playing with his ring.
He slept restfully with her for the first time in months.

The Klan Passes James By
Walking toward the campfire, the Dog saw the robed Klansmen first.
In the starlit open space, it was too late to hide.
The Dog stopped, stamping his right foot 13 times.
The stone in the ring around his neck began to glow.
James stood to the Dog's right recognizing the calling ritual
and lifted his arms and shouted the words that his father
had made him memorize when he was 5 years old:
"God is our refuge and strength…Be still, and know that I am God!"
The boy, the woman and the dog breathed as one
as the group of grand wizards passed them by.
Afterward, the woman asked to go her way alone but
James felt she had to be escorted: He owed her that much for her nice invite.

The Black Dog of Fate Smiles

"Where's ya family?" the woman asked seeing him fall asleep in her warm smile.
Dreaming his past and his future aloud, James told her about living in the big city
without being scared. "This was 1917! Things were happening in big cities!
He'd made her wear his old vest so she wouldn't be cold.
Waking at dawn and going back to thank his new colored friends,
James found an uninhabited, dilapidated mansion whistling the early morning chill:
Thinking, he musta got turned around, he followed her footprints.
The Dog and the boy made a sudden turn into a cemetery, stopping short, as
they both saw his vest carefully folded on a wild-flower covered grave
marked with, "Here lies Beloved, who guards the gates in spirit."
The Black Dog of Fate bowed as James just picked up his vest,
starting toward the train tracks and St. Louis Blues.

Country Watermelon

a sultry belly dancer
out of the way of the
vermilion green-stripped
quarter inch thick skin were
the exceptional pleasure

she moved in rolling waves
heavy laden vine
caesarian marks on her
a birthright that announced
of taste and texture

at her bleeding crimson heart

waiting to be revealed
harvested ripe and eaten
undulation of a full moon

as melon-honey
on a dirt path in the
in her season of beauty

Malcolm X

re-visiting **Time**
The Nothing that was
renames itself something
and we gasp listening to him
knowing *"Why We CAN'T Wait"*
watching you   fall on stage
organizational logic's decision
a conspiracy revealed to be
rhetorically incorrect
the discourse of murder
and protest synchronized
"Why Can't WE Wait"
as the minutes stand guard
over your body looking for the truth
and you turn your face to the wall
like a man
waiting for **Time**
to stop

TORNADO TALE
(for the Mississippi Belle & The Arkansas Timber Wolf but because of Ishmael Reed)

It is that Time of Spring again, as my 7 year old eyes sit
reading on the narrow iron porch.
The LOUP GAROU, who lives in the next apartment,
has returned once again as a giant bull bat hanging
from the porch roof in front of his door;
where the wind whips around the corner hard
and slams all the doors shut during a storm.
I wave to him 4 feet away and continue reading.

I am 25 feet in the air on the iron porch
and I can see the surrounding landscape before me;
That includes The TWISTER blowing in due south.
The pasty blue sky is slowly darkening
with low-hanging purple clouds.
The apartment's cat family enters the courtyard
in a fast walk, kitten in mouths in a hurry to get to the basement.
The Tom Cat meows an order to hurry up.
The building housed 40 families in a series
of 2 room apartments with toilet and sinks and
an untold number of cats and dogs in the basement.

My child's eyes see alternating lines of light in the distance.
I close my eyes and hear the lacerating sound of thunder.
The WIND is pushing the odometer and I am enjoying
the feeling of almost flight; of being free and clean
and as light as air.
Opening my eyes I see the storm sky has arrived.
All around me the celestial canopy is blurred
blue purple Cumulus clouds
rolling over each other in scary waves.
They are so near, so near, I think that I can walk on them.

The ornamental IRON PORCH is anchored in a concrete yard
surrounding the old brick building.
The Jews that own it, just had the gas jets for the lights
changed over to electric wiring.
Nannie's husband, The Giant BULL BAT
opens his wings hanging upside down
and swings in the wind;
When the birds in the trees stop singing.
Daddy's SPIRIT DOG races up the iron 60 step stairway
and says "Everything is okay: James will be here in a moment,"
peeks in the one door of the 2nd story apartment at Mama
cooking dinner and runs down the steps.
We ate supper with Daddy at exactly 5:00p.m. everyday.
Getting off the bus, Daddy in his summer Stetson,
shining Stacy Adams and starched white shirt
with the cuffs turned up, enters the courtyard,
as the rain starts to fall and things take to the air.

2 blocks up
The TWISTER
jumps the backyards
and starts walking
down the street
like a man;
escort lightning
bolts crashing
on its arms.
I remember thinking,
"Oh it's here- my ride…"
So I take a hold
of the clothesline
and slide from
the porch
to the pole
next to the house
across from
the courtyard

and I climb
onto the roof.
Lights go out
everywhere.
I am really
floating now:
almost airborne
as I hear people
screaming:
But I have found
a new space
to inhabit and
I am happy:
Like Dorothy
going to Oz
or wading in the water
at Bethesda, I am going
to be free.
The crack of lightning
penetrates my closed eyes
and the boom of the explosion
under my feet, makes me
fall forward into a taloned grip
Nannie's husband had me and
Daddy's SPIRIT DOG was on the
porch waiting for him to put me down.

I grab hold of the iron railing;
feet spinning in the air.
Terrified, everyone was huddling
locked in doors, as The TWISTER
whirled there for a moment
trying to uproot The IRON PORCH.
Lightning resounding through its poles
was grounded by hammered iron into a fizz that said,
"Ecurile, sha a la fea ne:
This one you will pass today, my brother."
Seeing the flying BLACK DOG next to me

The TWISTER answered, *"Adupe!*
She is already under my protection and we will
meet again," before spinning upwards
only to come down again and blow up the
houses on 4 sides of us.
"Why was this building spared?" everyone asked.

Sitting on the rickety wooden bench
only slightly amazed that the world is so weird,
my 7 year old eyes go back to The Giant BULL BAT
who scares people, The BLACK DOG that only
me and Daddy can see, and to reading my book,
in between viewing the clear pale sky following
in The TWISTER's aftermath.

CUENTRO DE EN TORNADO
(Spanish translation by Henry Mattison)

Llegó la primavera otra vez
mientras mis ojos de siete años
se sientan a leer en lo fresco del anochecer
en la estrecha entrada de hierro.
El LOUP GARROU que vive al lado
ha regresado otra vez disfrazado de
murciélago gigantesco colgado
en el techo de la entrada enfrente de su apartamento;
donde el viento sopla duro en la esquina
y cierra de golpe todas las puertas durante una tormenta.
Le agito la mano a cuatro pies de distancia y sigo leyendo.

Estoy a 25 pies en el aire en la entrada de hierro y puedo ver
todo el paisaje delante de mi;
Eso incluye El TORNADO que sopla del sur.
El azúl tranquilo del cielo pastoso delante de mi
se vuelve ve oscuro con nube púpuras oprimentes. Los gatos, unos
veinte, empiezan a pasearse en el jardín con el gato de papá
maullando que se apuren. Las Gatas llevan a sus gatitos en la boca
hacia el sótano de un edificio de concreto y ladrillo que aloja a
cuarenta familias en un serie de apartamentos de dos cuartos con
excusados y fregaderos.

Mis ojos de niña ven líneas alternativas de luz a la distancia. Cierro
los ojos ys escucho el ruido la cerante del trueno. El viento empuja
el odometro y disfruto la sensación de vuelo de ser libre, limpia y
liviana como el aire. Al abrir los ojos veo que el cielo tormenta ha
llegado. El dosel celestial es un azúl púrpureo borroso de nube
cúmulus revolcandose unas sobre otras como olas amenzantes.
Estan tan cerca que pienso poder caminar sobre ellas si tuviera una
escalera.

La ENTRADA DE HIERRO ornamental esta anclada en un
jardín de concreto donde crece mala hierba en las grietas durante
el verano. Los propietarios judíos acaban de cambiar los chorros de
gas para las luces a cable eléctrico. El marido de nanny, El
MURCIÉLAGO GIGANTESCO, abre sus alas colgadó al revés y se
balancea en el viento. Los pájaros en los árboles de jardín de al

lado paran de cantar. El "PERRO ESPIRITU" de papá sube de prisa los 60
escalones de la escalera de hierro y dice "Todo va bien: Jaime va a estar en va
momento" se asoma en la única puerta del apartamento, ve que mamá esta coci-
nando y baja las escaleras a prisa. Cenamos con papá a las cinco en punto
cada día. Bajándose del autobús, papá con su Stetson de verano,
stacey adams relucientes y una camisa blanca almidonada con las
mangas reojidas entra al patio cuando empieza a llover y las cosas
vuelan al aire.

Dos cuadras mas arriba
el tornado
salta los patios
y empieza
a caminar
calle abajo:
relampagos
caen con estrepito en sus
brazos.
Recuerdo pensar
"Oh! Aquí esta
mi viaje."
Agarro la cuerda
para tender la ropa
y me deslizo
de la entrada
hacia el poste
al lado de
la casa enfrente de mi
y subo al tejado.
Las luces se van por todo.
Estoy flotando, casi en el aire
y escucho que la gente grita
pero he descubierto un espacio
nuevo para vivir y estoy feliz; Como Dorothy que se va a oz
o caminando en agua en Bethesda,
finalmente voy a ser libre
cierro los ojos pero la luz del relampago
los penetra y el boom
de la explosion bajo mis pies

hace que me caigo boca abajo
hacia manos garras.
El esposo de nanny me sujetaba
y el perro de papá PERRO ESPIRITU
estaba en la entrada
esperando que el me soltara.

Agarro la barandilla de hierro
los pies dando vueltas en el aire.
Todos estaban espantados
amontonados detras de puertas enllavadas
mientras EL TORNADO giraba allí un momento
tratando de desarraigar la entrada de hierro.
El relampago resoñando
atraves de sus postes metálicos
fue martillado a un burbujeo que dijo:
"Escurile, sha a la fe a ne:
de ésta se salvará hoy, mi hermano."
Viendo el PERRO volaba junto a mi
el tornado contestó: *"Adupe!*
Ya esta bajo mi protección
nos volveremos a ver" antes de girar hacia arriba
solo para bajar otra vez y destruir las casas
alrededor de nosotros
"Porqué se salvó este edificio?"
Todo el mundo se preguntaba mas tarde.

Mientras la entrada de hierro silba
para hacerme compañía
sentada en el banco de madera tambaleante
solo un poco asombrada
que el mundo sea tan raro
mis ojos de siete añera se vuelven
hacia el murciélago macho gigantesco
que asusta a la gente, el PERRO NEGRO
que solo papá y yo podemos ver
y de vuelta a mi lectura
mientras veo el cielo claro y pálido
despues de las consecuencias de TORNADO.

The Heart Is A Lonely Hunter: Urse's Song/ Bess' Lament

What is Beauty
abandoned
in migrating molecules
that color what we feel?
What is Beauty as it exists
without enabling misery
to extend itself as Life
standing on a dark corner
with no father?
What is Beauty
if not experience's ability
to sculpt tissue in its dictation
of form and behavior:
telling itself that the show
must go on…go on?
Can we observe Beauty's ability
to lift despondency,
erase joblessness,
feed the hungry?
What is the Life that
She can no longer bear
one more moment nor forever, as
a wayward artist,
the dancer born a lone victim
as a woman in constant crisis
lost in the pain game of
abuse's custom tailored artistry?
What is Beauty in crushed flesh
flowering purple bruises
cut to fear on the clothesline
in a tornadoes path?
What exactly is Humanity
when what is humane is not possible
and so fragile a blonde-black blossom
is left wandering
in the blue moonlight
of a vampire's hunger?

Momma's Dancing Shoes' Blues
(because of Langston Hughes but for my shoe-shopping daughter)

The year is gone now
And I put my blues to rest
Year is gone now
And I put my blues to rest
Gonna take my dancing shoes out
And put them to the test

Love my blue shoes
They are lovely like the sky
Love my black shoes
They sing birdie bye and bye
Love my red shoes
They can send him floating high

Love my silver slippers
In them I can't do no harm
Love my white slippers
In them I charm away charm
In my gold slippers
I can out sparkle the sun

Dancing Dancing
Dancing in my dancing shoes
Dancing Dancing
Gonna dance away my blues
Ain't it funny how time flies
When you're moving in a groove

Laura Nyro Dances
(from *Odes to Ailey II*)

a **quintet**, they dance a spirit that leaves us drugged
in the poured on shiny red dresses
of Chinese, Black and White Supremes
mimicking Death in love me red high heels and
blonde Marilyn Monroe wigs
they blind us with their sequined light
at noon on a stone soul picnic with no food

they are us, we are them in our
skin dresses shaking memories of that
tantalizing early innocent kiss
on the church's stairway before
Lucky escaped our grasp
Escaped out little neighborhood
Saying, "Go get Lucky!"

I am them, they are me in my destitution
of spirit lost on the no where going
train of Time in non-material reality
no seat to sit upon, I stand through my hunger
stand through my thirst, stand through my vulnerability
living lives apart, the stops connect our addictions
on board the Poverty Train

you are not dreaming the haze of Xmas mania
or the depression of a happy new year
the one thing you can not give, will save you
in the resounding echo of your true name, the confession
of a lifetime that announces itself,
as a confrontation with evil that blinds us
in this dance of beauty that always leaves us drugged

The First Ho In Space
(for Captain James T. Kirk)

galvanized in
a saunter that
was wicked
in fashion-police approved
pirate boots
and a tacky t-shirt
hair lock in place
lips poised for
interstellar penetration
of federation proportions
Columbus faces his
alternate reality of progress
beyond 14th century aggrandized
testosterone delusions
run amok

El Primer Ho En El Espacio
(Spanish translation by Maya Gross and Henry Mattison)

galvanisado en
un deambular
cruel
en botas de pirata
aprobados
por la moda policíaca
y una camiseta destartalada
mecha de pelo en su lugar
labios preparados para
la penetración inter estelar
de proporciónes federales
colon se enfrenta con
su realidad alternativea del progreso
mas alla de los engaños
testosterónicos, agigantados
enloquecidos
del siglo 14

Blues For Josephine Baker

I see you
Can you see me
We can dance
Under the Banana Tree

                              St. Louis born
                              On the streets at 13
                              Singing and hustling
                              Against the poverty scene

Shuffle Along in 22'
Chocolate Dandies in 24'
Des Champs-Elysees
And Paris wanted more

                              Creole colored in mind
                              Though a tiger at heart
                              Separate but equal
                              Failed to give her a start

The Goddess had come
As magic survived
The Mumbo Jumbo Princess
Sensuality alive

                              So in Paris she stayed
                              A woman worshipped in the streets
                              On the back of an ostrich
                              Or walking her panthers on a leash

Writers love her
ee cummings too
Langston Hughes inspired
How she do what she do

                              Intelligence agent
                              Performer, mother of 12
                              The Legion d'Honneur
                              Le Croix de la Guerre

One man's dream
And another's to get
She hypnotized 4 husbands
Without missing a step

                        A writer, a fighter,
                        A dancer too
                        A legendary singer
                        To teach me the blues

I see you
Can you see me
We can dance
Under the Banana Tree

Strong Women Do Not Want To Keep A Man

The generation curse
of the men of the savanna
exposed her,
marched her,
made her undoing
her strength.
Made crossing continents
A priori:
Seeding life
In a hard enslavement
Learning new environments
A bitter segregation testing new ideas.

*"Mythmakers, blood carriers, moon-fairies,
women need protection."*

Hunters are important
for hunting game –
for protection
in Africa, Australia,
India, Wall Street,
Harvard Yard,
the Pentagon and
in the ghetto:
hunting for meat – not vegetables
hunting first with rocks and then
with bows, arrows, guns and
words: hunting to keep her covered
with the warmth that brings
a child's kiss, pregnant:
hunting drunk like
Cupids high on
opened cough syrup
in Baltimore or
refined sugar in Cuba –
numb.

"Chiefs of Earth and Sky, monarchs of Destiny,
emperors of Industry, men need control."

She watched them march,
on their way to sniffing cocaine and
yet another drive-by shooting.
She watched them
wailing, like Parker
screaming like horns
with no players.
She watched them
walk pass the water
into the desert
and holding the hand
of her child,
she took a stand for the survival of her kind.

The Mayor Of Gilmor Street

                        Arching his back
                    in an acquired grace
                the Mayor of Gilmor Street
            peruses the four corners
                    of his kingdom
                    with the visual acuity
                    of a warrior with second sight.

                            A veteran born and bred
                        in Union Square,
                    he'd surrendered his life
            to the historical conflicts
                    that drive evolution along
                    the Mason-Dixon Line.

                                Borderlands on Lombard and Pratt
                            circumcised the sanctity of peace
                    gone awry. For the moment,
                    all was quiet on the Eastern Front.
                    No "lost boys" on the corner.
                    No screaming fire trucks
                    saving the community.
                    No dreaming hippies
                    religious fanatics
                    campaign workers
                    or dope demons
                    hanging out;
                    just a couple
                    shooting up
                    in the alley
                    among
                    the used
                    condoms
                    next to
                    the ugly
                    iron gate.

                        This was a good day,
                    with smiling skies
                and purified air
                waltzing with manicured trees.
                Unicorns circle the park's interior
                and post-Victorian maidens
                glitter, twirling their parasols,

passing the row of aging
over-priced mansions.
The Union Army could have rested
easily here at Mencken's
Fountain of Virtue
        Today.

                    Nevertheless, the Mayor found
Pratt Street's anomalies more
unreasonable, more unsolvable.
Homeless people, an unfinished pocket park,
more tacky renovation work, desperate little children,
garbage and scores of boarded-up buildings;
            What was he to do?

He called the City
but nothing's likely to change
before the Garden Tour.
He doesn't know the answer;
            But he knows that he has a responsibility
to try to help them.
His house is a cultural presence
in a ghetto of immense exactitude.
His husband almost understood
what this meant but not quite…
The strange Black Man next door
is coming out. The Mayor says
"I just want to tell you…"
The neighbor listens before
signifying about people
throwing grass seed in his yard and

then languidly strolls away.
The Mayor shakes his head
in understanding
watching him bend to kiss the
Weird Black Woman up the street.
The Mayor had helped her
move into her home.

       "Is it possible that Acts of Charity
       have their own reward?" he thinks,
       closing town hall by
       ascending the marble steps
       towards the softness of his lover's voice
       in the dusky light of
       a noisy summer night.

Wind In The Cane XII

I feel your tallness
inside my mind,
as clouds rise higher
to read your thoughts.
I am liquid fire,
timeless Amber
in the kettle of
your burning hands,
turned slightly to make
the reach
to the place I want
to be
naked, in the slip-sliding joy
of your love.

Rodin's "The Thinker" Reflects On Lynching As A National Past-Time

in my city   ebony naked singing hymns
what's the sound   me thinks he thinks
too much   of the past rock
that is still   the present foundation

poem this   thinking digitally
counting if you can   dead men, women and children
the long walk   from redwood, cedar and magnolia trees
               to Pratt Street

I think you think   about such beautiful furniture
too much about   segregated society at twilight
            when it's hard to see the
red black and green beaded blood
                our kind tasted on the whip
we think they think   on a millennium dawn
                       Maybe

just thinking isn't enough

The Labyrinth
(for Nancy Romita, dancer & choreographer)

the Ring of Fire
meets
the Ring of Hope
in a search
for wholeness
to be acted out in
a Walk of Faith
in metaphorical space
that transmutes energy
within and without
in the Dance of an
ancient soul

Cowboy Surgeon
(for Dr. Nikita Levy with thanks)

Motorized urban buckaroo
   he straps on his six-shooters
   argues with the insurance company's
   anti-patient ontology, before
   gearing up to do battle with invaders in
   fashionable immaculate green duds
   accented by brown mules.
   Properly gloved, he
   heads on out for a long day's ride
   in the operating saddle.

Marvin Gaye sings,
  "You're so great,
  I can't wait for you to operate..."
  That's what he says.

Stethoscope in one hand
patient file in the other
he wearily saunters the corridors
between the operating room
and recovery hall as a king
juggling lives and life times
like marbles against the
unfathomable mysteries
of the feminine form he celebrates.

Entering Into The Beginning Of Myself

in the wells of your arms
grow the mad sea strains
of lost fishermen lives
ever long, ever enduring
as The river keeps her promise

set in the stone of flesh
that abides human frailty
I leave the past on the shore
with the truth and swim out
to the whirlpool

blue to black to blue
my svelte nakedness
in the dark shining
you are me when I am I
that which we are we are

a shared net of gossamer
entraps us in our severed embrace
where in the wells of your arms
I lose the dream springing from your eyes
sinking, I ride the waves holding on

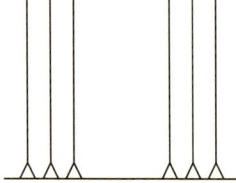

Clarinda Harriss

"I am The Voice of the Past that will always be
I am The Voice of your hunger and pain,
I am The Voice of the Future
I am The Voice, I am The Voice…"

"The Voice" sung by Eimear Quinn
On *Faire Celts: A Woman's Voice*
Words & music by Brendan Graham
Acorn Music Ltd./Peer Music Ltd.
Compact disc by Narada World Productions 2000

BONDO

Be wary
Of that guy who knows how to paint
New shine over old parts. The
Doors may be rusty, the renders made of glue.

Oh, he'll tell you it's a
Rare find, one of a kind,

Better than new, and who cares what the
Odometer says?
No use kicking the tires, you're going to buy it,
Drive it home, pump gas into it,
Open it up on the freeway till it quits on you.

My Claustrophobic Valentine

You know, don't you,
that by hating closed space
as much as I do
you greatly increase

the chances of your
getting stranded with me
in an elevator.
I only go upstairs when the

guy's right, that is, when
there's something major
we have in common.
You hate heights, I hear.

Me too. That puts us
at sea level in a three-sided hut,
preferably made of grass.
Margarita, love?

Thunder

They also serve who only stand and jeer:
that seemed to be the theory of the boys haunting
Mom's Diesel Stop and Convenience Store
on Route 50 in '52. So what if we were flaunting
whatever budding bumps and nubbins jabbed
though our size-S shirts. It was a lightning
revelation, how our mere passing hocked up gobs
of spit from deep in their gut till strings
of mumbles dripped from the corners of their mouths.
How many years before it would dawn
on us that people actually did, for love,
what the truckstop jockeys claimed
they had in mind for us, I wonder–
or what real tenderness drowned in diesel thunder.

Babel

Ten days in England and English turned foreign,
black headlines blaring FRANCE HAVE WON,
BRAZIL ARE OUT all over the London Times,
baps oozing fat rashers in the fast-food chains.
We began to forget the American words for things
like bonnets, boots, lounges, roundabouts, slip roads,
and the sweet milky tea that had almost out-cappucinoed
Seattle when we left the States.
                              "What's that thing?"
you whispered when flight attendant walked the aisles
at westward take-off dangling a lost bag. "Knapsack?"
I murmured, but I knew the term wasn't much more right
than "hold-all," which is what the British Airways boychild
called it. Soon as the plane began to clamber up the night
one lost word returned: Chai: what we Yanks call that drink.

Our heads hung heavy, motion's shrieky babble tamed
by Dramamine. You mumbled your ex-wife's name.

After The Baby Funeral

> *"I've got all the time in the world"*
> —*Mark Sandman, "Radar," from Morphine's 1995 CD "Yes"*

> *"I don't care how dead he is, he's the sexiest man alive"*
> —*overheard in a record shop (referring to Mark Sandman)*

It was juice, jazz, joss, jissm we called
on for comfort (gospel of response/recall)
after the little white box

we couldn't and couldn't not
look at in the church
was lowered into dirt for the leaching of its linen

Dead babies play at the feet of Jesus
or so the preacher oiled us, but
dead boys played on the stereo

rock-hard while we cooked and fucked
as if we needed meat to replenish the flesh the savage
god exacted

CRABFINGERS

Red new hooks are growing
on my foreknuckles--
middle age did it, nibbling
at my tips.
Overhead paddles the Goodyear Blimp,
so close I feel
I could poke its soft keel
with a forefinger.

The water is dark down here,
warm and salty.
No rush, no rush. Down here, but
deeper, my father
lies, mostly bones now. Crabfingers
picked him clean
before he died, saving the sweet
brain for last.

From a tin packed on the shore
of the Chesapeake,
crabfingers poke out claws; I lick
their genital scent
off my own stiff fingers
and swallow.
No rush, no rush. There's many
a husk to suck.

Now across a picnic table
under Baltimore air
July-heavy and a full five fathoms
deep in heat,
my lover's fingers hook the steel
and gut strings
of his guitar, carefully picking out
a song,

one plump chunk at a time.

Spendthrift

> *Spindrift, n.. Spray blown from a rough sea or surf.*
> *"The mountainous seas crashed down upon our decks, and the stinging, wind-driven spindrift burned its way into our flesh."* —Vaughn.
> *[Webster's New Unabridged Dictionary]*

I hate the word "squander"
but I love the way you do it,
the way you cast your gold
into the wind and it flies

back in our faces as mist, but
no, not so cold: as buttery salt,
melted and lovely to lick.
With you standing over me

naked, half-lit by hall light
I think of your father tending
the open hearth at the steel mill
in his woollen shirt,

 the fibers kinking like hair
in the hundred-forty-five heat
while the molten slag set
the Patapsco River on fire

every Baltimore midnight
near where Moran's tugboats
worked and rich people's
sailboats lay at anchor.

I think of your sailboat,
how I never met it but still
feel it under me sometimes,
a phantom leg of the Bay.

On the wide white deck
of your bed I've felt the sea crash
and the wind-driven spindrift burn
its way into my flesh.

HE CAN. SHE CAN.
(for Dick from Clarinda, December 31, 1999)

A man may love a woman
because she can sing along,
around and over (but not too high or well)
his grumblesome baritone.

A woman may love a man
because he can tell at one glance
which leftover will fit into which freezer bowl,
this one or that one.

A man may love a woman
because she's always right
except when it comes to right versus left. He can
follow her anywhere. No one else can.

A woman may love a man
because he can do this
dumbfounding thing to the back of her neck
with his thumbs.

A woman may love a man
because sometimes running on
nothing but heart and tongue he can still love her
all night long.

A man and woman may love
each other till death does them done
because he can dance, and she can too,
when Ella croons.

Lost Dog Possibilities

He ran off with your ex-husband
or a pack of feral butterflies disguised as
the red/gold flash of a setter bitch .

He's been taken in by a pair of slick
Siamese who flatter him with their attention
to every little flick of his tail.

It's his mission to help the elderly
cross streets. Once they get their crabbed claws
in his fur they hold on for blocks, like burrs.

A tick has sucked out every drop of him.
He's nothing but an empty leather purse
attached to a giant purple balloon.

Thinner, he is, than the limp yellow
Xeroxed flyer that cries his loss from lamppost
to lamppost, from March to September.

He's holed up in Voyeurdorm.com with Becky
"We're not whores" and Kim "Whatever." You can
hear him howl at the moony ceiling cams.

He's hiding in a longbed truck's extended cab.
He's living in the outback wondering what
jackals act like. He's dead on a front bumper.

He's flying on coppery wings through cerulean
blue, panting and slobbering eternally, but
never begging. Retrieving, not fetching.

He never loved you.

Hauling the Dog

80 pounds of aching
dog dangle from my arms
at the level of my bent knees.
Four stone steps down to go before she pees.

There's a despairing
moment of hairy balance
when each of us ungainly bitches
wrestles against the headlong pitch

and wins. Her blood sinks
back from her trembling skin
to her bandaged limb. I cool down
too. For a second I imagine that I've joined

the mothers who grab
Volkswagens by the bumper and
heave them off struck children, full
of crazed adrenalin. Or the boy who lifted his pet bull

every day since it was born
till the baby Angus weighed five
hundred pounds. Or the girl who propped
a wall with her body till the earthquake stopped.

Wings of hormones,
angels of brute patience,
that we can summon them is no more
wonderful than going down any flight of stairs--

juggling our bones
in the grave and weighty air,
with each step for a deadly second
we cast all our weight on neither of our legs

and make our way,
neither flying nor falling,
easy in the muscle hug that holds
on hard to dog, to car, to calf, to child.

Numina

I've always been ambivalent about revenants,
the way they stare into the refrigerator
with its small light stunning their eyeglass lenses
blind while cold air thickens all around them.
And that awful thing they do at the far end of the night
-lit hall just as I step out of the bathroom.

Still it's good to see them, good they come
around, telling their old stories in their old voices.
and bring a repertoire of new tricks along.
I'm amazed the way my father runs
through every passport photo face he ever wore
quick as riffling a pinochle deck, how Grandma
quit the Church for silvery Mae West curves and clothes.
I think love among the living shakes them.
My ghosts come around less now I have an old man
they approve of. My friend's dead son stopped
coming home on weekends when she married again.

Yet there must be things ghosts forget they'd forgotten.
Even the dead dogs lug their grudges into the house
to puddle the rug in their former corners
and trouble the new dog's muffled breathing
as she sleeps curled up in her numinous pen.

Boss Mama's Funeral

The dog is not present
        in that
      she was disposed of   by the Falls Road Animal Hospital.

The dog is not present
        in that
      there is no logical end   to the airy arc of a biscuit.

The dog is not present
        in that
      food on the floor is scarfed up   by the smallest children.

The dog is not present
        in that
      the smallest children are back   at the bottom of the Being-Pole.

The dog is not present
        in that
      the larger children refuse   to wash their hands, saying there's no reason.

The dog is not present
        in that
      the older less continent   people have no one
      but   each other to identify with.

The dog is not present
        in that
      we know now   the noises in the house are made by ghosts.

The dog is not present
        in that
      what we have left   is a tin Milkbone box with her old hairy collar
          and nameless tags (she had no vanity) which we will now bury
          under the witch hazel tree.

The dog is not present
        in that
      box.

Pit Bull Owl

I. The Question

My darling, my wise old bird
man, you were very comforting
when I told you in the morning
I'd spent all last evening
with my old gone dog sleeping
between my window and bed: you said
owls make that deep breathing
sound as well and once you'd heard
it yourself. What you couldn't tell
me was why a pit bull
came back in the form of an owl.

(Your explanation was soothing,
but so was her breathing.)

II. Boss Mama Answers

        Pit bull

                growls

owl

        howls

                            fur

                                          brindled

                       feathers

                                  brindled

       sleep

              day

wake

         dark

                            owl

                                    bull

                    can't

                            smile

      bad luck

            to young?

wrong

        wrong

                          bull

                                owl

                  love

                       all   small

                        Bull gone
                                        all
        but smell
                        in rug

                                                        and paw-

                                                                fall
                                                                        in dark
                                                                hall

                        or owl's
                                        low
                growl
                                soft

                                                soft   soft   soft   soft

Local Fauna

Lively, yes, but nothing's lovely under the Chesapeake,
prettiness can't live in that silt.
Crabs in heat do an idiot gavotte and make blue babies.
Those washed-up horseshoe
shells have a Vehrmacht helmet look, and what
are those vile
sucker-guts that get stuck to our insteps?
The flexing mussels
are less iridescent than a mechanic's oily blue coverall
or oil on asphalt.
Porpoises' cartoon monkeyshines stir up dirty foam.

Only sometimes

when a white late-summer dime of sun
dribbles a stream
of powdery light through the junk and murk, you see
some pale translucent
jelly waft like Loe Fuller's blooming silks, writhe
like ghosts of smoke
over Sonny Stitt's and Sonny Rollins' steaming saxes
in the whiskey-brown
velvet deeps of the Red Fox Club, circa 1960,
down there
next to the Tijuana Lounge on Fulton Street.

The Stand-off

Everyone hugs his own theory
about what went wrong in Dundalk:
revenge and unrequited love,
time not served, bad medicine,

those taunts as old as childhood
everyone hugs. The killer's own theory
shapes a romance. Not for him,
revenge, nor unrequited love!--

he could have anyone he wanted!
Taunts as old as childhood
curl his 4-day-bearded lip.
Shapes a romance—not for him—

hint at move behind drawn blinds.
He could have anyone he wanted.
Below, police with cell phones
curl his 4-day-bearded lip

with their groveling Misters and Sirs.
He hints his moves behind drawn blinds
or so it seems to the TV crews.
Below, police with cell phones

catch naps in vans or practice
their groveling Misters and Sirs.
Daily life spins in a loop
Or so it seems to the TV crews.

Hostage to the screen we yawn,
catch naps in vans or practice
our swing with phantom clubs.
Daily life spins in a loop

we feel we've known forever,
hostage to the screen. We yawn,
sleep, eat, shave, dress, pretend
our swing with phantom clubs

could make us heroes.
We feel we've known forever
these strangers who seem to need us.
We sleep, eat, shave, pretend

what went wrong in Dundalk
had nothing to do with us, our
time not served, bad medicine
we swallowed with first milk.

At Camden Yards

Look at that woman over there.
Who'd wear an outfit like that to a baseball game!

> Satin top, teeny pleated skirt--
> like my old ballet school's costumes.
> Long fine bones, wide painted eyes--
> she could be a dancer--

Look down there. ED-DY! ED-DY!
Murray's going to hit his 500th home run.
There it goes! Yes!

> What's she got, a tiny video cam?
> No, a regular camera so ancient
> it's a fat black box with a kind of nozzle.

Why doesn't that bitch sit down.
Goddam confetti. Look at the mess on the field.

> Thousands of gold paper streamers shine
> brighter than the strange grass
> in this unnatural light. Look! the grounds
> crew is trying to pick them up one by one.

Why doesn't that bitch sit down.
Doesn't she know she's blocking the view?
Doesn't she know the wind is about to
blow that little skirt up over her ass?

> Look how adoringly her husband throws his arms
> around her thighs to protect her modesty
> while she snaps that perfect picture.
>
> Such a parade of conditions I can never aspire to.

OH: A FOOTNOTE ON THE HISTORY OF DAMITA JO
Singer, 1930-1998

Oh Damita, Oh Damita Jo
You can't be dead. Oh no.
We loved you here in Baltimore.
Nineteen fifty-four or so
some skinny grit I used to go
out with drove up from Alabama for your show.
We danced till the sidelines echoed
Go ! Go! Go!
Afterwards he tried to explain blow
jobs, you know,
it wasn't really sex if this didn't go
into that, o-
kay? I was a slow
learner. So....

"Performing in beaded, handmade gowns, Miss Jo
headlined at major clubs and ho-
tels and made recordings popular in Japan and Puerto Rico."
Monday, December 28, 1998: it said so
in the Baltimore Sun. "Take a Little Lone-
liness," you sang on the Steve Allen show.

Married through your Mo-
town years, I chose
loneliness, or at least divorce. '79, the year you so-
loed with Ray Charles at Tow-
son State–I don't know why I didn't go
to hear you–I taught there lo
those many years ago and, in fact, do so

still. Your face glows in the obituary photo.
You look like a darker Marilyn Monroe.
Back then I tried to also.
Pretty sisters–though
you and Marilyn should have let me know
you were about to die so
I could phone you or something, you know?
Well, as that dumb saying goes,
when you gotta go you gotta go.
Go! Go! Go! Damita Jo.

SUMMER: TIME

to sing of Jute
god of sailors, god of knots, god of hammocks

to sing of Bite
god of gin, god of singing wings

to sing of Bolt
god of get inside quick, god of ionized dark

to sing of Wet
goddess of salt licks sea-big or armpit-little

to sing of Rot
god spawned in a shoe by Wet and Time

to sing of Clink
god of cool sweat

to sing of Fuzz
goddess of the sheen on things

to sing of Girls
"Early" and "Cherry" the red-light vestals

to sing of Ripe
that sanctified slut with her big hot knockers.

Weeding

They say it's good
for you, but just
in case we are what we eat
you'd best believe

I'm never going to eat
purslane--
pusillanimous fat crawler
always sucking up

to my tomatoes, corn, peppers,
spinach, lettuce.
Only eat what you respect.
Cannibals know.

Pretty Roquette has gone
bitter, bolted,
sunk to purslane's level
like some slug

that won't even drink beer
and die. Heat's
jazzed this city like an old-
fashioned cathouse

and I'm with the working girls,
Early Girl, Silver
Queen, Sweet Roma. Call me Ruby.
Ruby Chard.

Mozart Night: At The Meyerhoff::
Stains On A Long White Dress

Mozart: Rondo for Flute in D Major.
The pretty floutist may be six months pregnant.
She looks medieval with her long white dress
floating over the oval bulge below her breasts.
She wipes her mouthpiece on a lacy fold
of skirt. The audience licks its lips.

Horn Concerto No. 2 in E-flat Major.
Allegro. Hounds burble in the distance.
In the foreground, birds. Something dies
during the Andante that follows--horse,
rider, dog or bird. The soloist stands helpless
in his perfect summer tux. Some wild flesh bleeds
through a torn-off strip of thin white cloth.

Bassoon Concerto in B-flat Major
The cellists, now divorced, bow their fiddles
side-by-side. Once a Hungarian refugee, he
dolls his bald head up in an invisible bandage,
slightly bloody, a girl's torn-off lace dress,
so dramatic! She has resumed her maiden name.
She bleeds discreetly under her white dress.
During the Adagio she imagines him wound
in thin white cloth from pate to foot.
Her cramps subside. Her low tones ripen.

Symphony 41 in C Major, "Jupiter"
The audience can hardly wait to clap
and yell foreign words. They've been dying
to get into the act for hours. If
the big jugs of red wine were here
instead of in the lobby the men imagine
they'd pour it all over the women's
long white dresses and lap it
out of their laps. . .Some of the women
imagine a man's head under their long
white wine-stained skirts, maybe Mozart's.

"Sundial," 410-783-1800

I recalled the Gullah woman
my father used to tell me about
who could sing two notes at once
one in her throat one in her mouth
so I dialed the "Sample" number
in italics under a Baltimore Sun article
on Huun-Huur-Tu the Throat-Singers
from Tuva on the edge of Mongolia
who are appearing at the Smithsonian
and yes somebody from a long way away
sang double right over the phone
and then they did a number
called "evengileer" "whose pulsating
rhythm is said to evoke
the sound of a cantering horse"
and it was true the hooves
barely touched down the rocking
would make you seasick
if it weren't so fast and close
to earth with the rider's own
thighs feeling it to the bone
my father would have felt it
the same way he always heard
trotting carriage horses in
most of Vivaldi and all of Bach
and then they sang in praise
of a Tuvan city which was clearly
rainy and full of alley-pools
that swam with rainbows like Paris
back in the early 30s when my father
drank "decent cheap wine" there
during the tail-end of Prohibition and
I wished my father could dial
this number until I realized

I had dialled my father

something I'd been trying to do
ever since he died in 1989.

Union Memorial Hospital

Packed with naked bodies in every posture
of adandon, this must be the most
antisexual place in the world tonight,
this wheezing, dozing hospital
where every half-open door reveals
a waxen homunculus in a bed
that resembles a torture instrument
or a significant other strewn over
a reclining chair like discarded clothes.
Awful holes emitting snores or apparatus.
Worst, the parodies of veins suspended
in clear plastic tubing from above
while parodies of bowels gnarl around bedlegs.
I walk the halls dragging a yellow bag.

A persistent friction, the tug of a tube
scotchtaped to my crotch

    must, therefore, explain why
    in this Temple of Anaphrodisia I
    find I'm counting myself to sleep
    with old lovers' names, counting how many
    love positions the mechanical
    bed could twist a body into
    by the right touch
    of the Head Foot Up Down buttons,
    finally counting the flourescent stars
    in the sexy downtown skyline--
    having thrown the drapes back from
    the wall-size window in my room
    to give the whole city a wink at
    my backless nightgown.

Downtown Hot September

Sirens split sullen air, share a long sigh
with people hunched on stoops.
Certain parts of the city still
simmer with summer.

Keisha sitting on my knee.

Mist hovers over the harbor, smoky
heather-blue, hot and heavy as swamp gas.
Evening heaves and rolls over,
fitful in fevered sleep.

One minute talking, kissing on me
(Gamma, she call me Gamma)
next minute slump over.

Sweat shimmers on every surface.
Tonight people risk a photo op in THE SUN
for the smallest rift
in air so solid it must be bulletproof.

Shot make no noise except sort of a hiss.

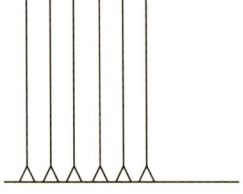

Kendra Kopelke

"...Her hair is Harlow gold
  Lips sweet surprise
  Her hands are never cold
  She's got Bette Davis Eyes..."

Performed by Kim Carnes
On *Mistaken Identity*
Written by Donna Weiss & Jackie DeShannon
EMI-America, 1981
Produced by Val Garay

Carpe Diem, Ants

Ants will drop whatever it is
  they're doing
  and follow one another
      with mary-tyler-moore-like enthusiasm

into a stranger's house, to seize
  a broken-
  off hunk of food, fifty times
      their size, pulling their stage coaches around in a

tight circle, or fortress, marking
  their trail with
  cartographic vigor.
      Arms and legs glued to the task before them, heads bowed,

they work with Mennonite patience,
  and will lift
  each crumb to their robed heads,
      their unfailing mandibles ready to take charge. Should one

stray from the herd, he or she will
  run top speed
  across the counter, the small
      heart sounding with the electronic frenzy of a

tripped security system. Split
  seconds count.
  A frightened ant can be a
      pathetic sight, racing about as if having

landed on the wrong planet,
  more angst than
  ant, sweating it out in full
      view of the enemy, huffing and puffing

with an innocence that vindicates
  him or her
  from any crime,
      which is why it makes it so difficult to kill

these untamed desperadoes
   once they pull
      the cord on their white flags. There
         is only so much the heart can undertake, only

so much will one can inflict in
   the arbi-
      trary ownership of one's
         house, in the space of an impressive afternoon watching

ants bloom in sharp black petals
   on the floor
   all because something has
      fallen from the heap, an accident, a stroke of luck.

Box Turtle

Usha was going to let it go
but my daughter and I wanted it
for a pet. I thought it might
round out our family, someone
we could both love;
it could be the man.
I would study its animal behavior,
observe its shell and famous turtle neck,
come to an understanding.
That night my daughter
and I went out to a party
and left the turtle in a box
on the dining room table.
When we came home,
I could hear, from the entryway,
the ragged beating against the cardboard,
begging, even in our absence,
and not for us.
I pictured a dark mound,
the weight of unhappiness,
a trumpeter's mute to hold in pain,
or worse, something alive
and powerless.
When I lifted him up
in an empty bonding gesture,
his legs pulled hard at the air;
I could see he was a strong swimmer,
a fast climber, someone who could manage
to get himself stranded in the middle
of a busy intersection.
While we slept there was great commotion—
the turtle fought valiantly
to climb out of the box,
rejected the lettuce
we offered. Before breakfast,
we let him go, then waited while
he sat in the dewy grass,
and sat some more,
head out and sweeping back and forth.
Not moving towards anything.
Not giving us one way to congratulate
ourselves for setting him free.

Annual Exam

It is cold as a Burger King meat locker
where I take my clothes off
and wait for a doctor I've never seen.
The gown the nurse flops on the table's
no surprise, pale blue crosses on white cloth,
like stitched doll's eyes, and my face
in the mirror looks just as wan
as it always does in these rooms,
my long hair stringy and lacking style.
A shy knock and she's in,
beautiful in her red batiked dress
and silver beads, thick black hair
pulled to a pony tail, a folder in her arms
like a score. She doesn't seem
interested in my self-diagnosed
good health, only the long line of deaths
that has preceded me—
Aunt Eileen and Uncle Keith, Pop, Grandma Florence,
what kind of diabetes by grandfather had,
and how young my great aunt was
who died of lung cancer,
how many heart attacks,
what year for the by-pass.
I sort out the diseases,
bride side and groom,
hoping some of what I tell her is true.
The list of the dead fills the chilly room,
my bony toes turn blue.
She extracts a lot of blood,
a faint *pffft* makes me dizzy
as the genes pile into the tube
taped with my last name.
Off to the lab, where God will factor
in the factors and print out the code.
Which death will be mine?

City Rooster

A healthy crow can dislodge a morning
from its sleepy dawn, let loose
the moorings, its throaty

anthem filling the sky with notes plucked out
like small seizures. Its speech
takes natural precedence,

like the high school music teacher
who always manages to sing
above the din:

sparrow, mocking bird, squirrel,
starling, junco, the heaves
and hos

of the garbage truck, now a muddle
of small talk. After lunch, when the day has
settled into itself,

the crows make their grand entrance on the road
in shiny black limousines, looking too much
like us as they step

on asphalt, flat-footed, unmoved by speeding
traffic. They stop to dine on a discarded
bag of fries or cheese

whopper, and jerk heartily, never minding the ketchup
mustache or mayonnaise ooze crusting
their beaks.

Having had enough, they unfurl cape-like wings
and jump, no, pull themselves up above the cars,
into sky,

swinging their torsos the way gymnasts mount
the higher bar. One will land on a nearby
street lamp, a long steel

arm hanging like a sentence over the highway, and watch
the sun darken the buildings and trees.
Then, out it comes,

the battered song, the flip side of an old 45,
*How Come Every Time I Itch I End Up
Scratching You,*

raw, animal, wild, falling in chunks to the ground,
a tune each of us knows
by heart.

Dogs

In this complex we walk
three or more times a day, my dog knows the bases
of things, the undersides of bushes,
the slender legs of the mailbox,
the lamp post's invisible scribble.

Tell me what you find, I wish I could ask him,
but nature insists we find things out for ourselves,
gives him no means for telling.
Today, after we had looked over a draft
of his poem, a shy student told me how it began

with depression, so severe, he couldn't leave the house,
or eat, or speak, and then vague feelings
surfaced, a man doing things
to a boy. Maybe the boy was his friend, he thought
at first, but no, maybe he was the boy,

he knew too much not to have been,
or maybe he dreamt the whole thing up,
because it acted like a dream, characters moving into
his neighborhood, changing places without warning.
Maybe the man was his neighbor, or his father,

it might have been his father, but he can't be sure,
and he doesn't care. He talked quietly under his
baseball cap, half child, half adult, like the dog nosing
intelligently the dry blades of grass, unable to
bring out anything to show for his trouble, not a stick,

a paper cup, the dusty heap of bird beneath a bush.
How is it we have these tracking devices in our bodies,
the sexual betrayals hunt us down, then loom, hidden,
afraid to reveal themselves to us? Or do we hunt them,
unconsciously, to have it out with them?

A male dog will pee every chance he gets,
practically turning himself inside out,
to mark another tree, and another, on its way.
As if there comes a point beyond which the body must
empty itself, separate from need; it creates its own

drive into oblivion: the man takes the boy,
and the boy takes to his head, describes himself simply
as dead. Later, poems begin to form inside him
and he says he doesn't know where they come from,
but he is curious about them,

more curious than he has been for a long time,
he writes himself back onto page,
each word a new scent,
he breathes slowly,
touching each sound.

Eating Out

What I like is the smell of coffee and
how a tuna sandwich with mayo on
soft whole wheat or toasted rye

comes to your table after only
a few words spoken to a stranger.
I like how it fits into your mouth

when you bite down, gingerly,
tearing off a discreet amount,
the rest of your body in an unembarrassing

position, no anxiety when
the teeth and tongue take over
in heavy rhythms and uninterrupted

precision. Then the spontaneous release
of miniature yelps inside the mouth,
a drama inside your head, your tongue

the stage, you chew, swallow,
chew, masticate, tongue directing
the meal around to patient molars

and brazen bicuspids.
You are having a good time,
the sandwich is filling you up in squishes

and gushes, some lands on your lip or chin,
the tongue sweeps it back inside.
You drink, talk occasionally, at ease.

Then the meal is over.
You put down a few dollars,
some extra for a tip, and walk back to your job

smelling of grease and secondary smoke,
clothes still on.

Elegy For The Cigarette

Behind Fair Lanes, on the back porch,
        or leaning against a pale blue Pontiac—,
                you escorted us through treacherous

years like an old family dog
        whose smells we absorbed in our clothes.
                You were a way out and the way

in, a small opening large enough to blow rings
        up to God and the next world,
                a crawl space of desire, the sigh

we called home. You taught us how to
        talk to one another
                about important things,

and the rhythm of silence,
        taught our bodies what boys would
                later teach who had become men,

how to crave things that were bad,
        that might kill us. Ask any smoker,
                in a world of want and plenty,

you were worth dying for.
        In singularity, circularity,
                with the shy innocence of a pencil,

you are now the object
        of such scorn and ridicule,
                a woman wearing fur, a man with a

weed whacker. Smokers loiter
        outside their office buildings,
                ghosts of their former sexiness.

At Spring Grove, the patients on the
        locked ward sat cross-legged
                in front of tv and chain smoked

till the cows came home. They didn't
    appear to know if they were
        awake or asleep,

only that a cigarette burned for them.
    You were all they cared about,
        were what they cared about,

cared more for you than
    their own fingers, stained
        with tobacco and blood.

Amidst urine smells, sudden screams,
    beds so public men slept
        in their clothes and shoes

so nurses wouldn't steal them
    you rose above it all—
        the great white breath

of sanity. O, ravishing star,
    tell us, how can we live
        with ourselves on earth,

in difficult times,
    what will we reach for
        to light our way?

Ode At The End Of The Century

In the movies,
on the streets,
in office buildings,
between loved ones,
everyone said fuck a lot,
it sat on the tongue
like the colored uniforms we wore
in gym class.
Fuck school, fuck you,
we'd say,
this fucking job,
fucking xerox machine, fuckin donuts,
you fucked up mother fucker,
a mantra swirling, spilling,
it plunged through the city
like ivy wearing a thicker
and thicker hide,
fuck was in the
bottle of ketchup,
fuck in the light on the leaves,
fuck on a moonlit night,
boats rocking in the harbor,
mothers in the kitchen,
girls in the cafeteria, before bras,
before cool, instead of cigarettes,
after toilet training and stacking colored cups,
pounded out as fast as babies
are born, free, portable,
microwavable,
I fucking love you,
I am so fucking happy,
the song at the end of the world.

Squirrel-O-Mania

You ought to be in therapy,
   the way you race about non-stop
      without looking where you are going,

always late,
   or smelling the hot breath
      of a predator that nobody sees but you,

then burying your peanuts in flower pots,
   like it's 1932, like you're a Depression baby,
   like you're everybody's favorite

eccentric relative, a little swishy.
   You shouldn't have been so easy-
      going when the migration

began, flexible diet, cooperative,
   impressed with human ambition,
      (I'm only guessing)

look where it got you, a shady cast
   of colleagues—pigeons, starlings,
      cockroaches, rats, tail-chasing rottweilers

and hissing cats.
   On good days I hear you
      leaping across the porch roofs

and I think Mozart, that's Mozart
   up there, the narcotic of joy, and joy riding,
      where movement is transposed

freely into song. Such a fine line you walk
   between joie de vivre and mania (people
      take Ritalin for the latter nowadays

to help them connect
   with their inner lives) you're too far out there
      playing the edges,

I look through my window
    at your blurry stride and think
        you can get away with murder

in this city but you cannot get away
    with cute, you come off looking like a true
        nut case, like your tail is what you keep

running from. I know, I know,
    things have picked up around here lately,
        daily rounds of shots, sirens,

police helicopters and car alarms,
    hypo-allergenic security systems,
        traps set everywhere,

but you've got to realize
    it's us we're after, not you,
        we're having it out with

human nature, and don't even hear
    the racket anymore. Fear
        is big business in Baltimore,

booby-trapped houses and cars,
    sensor lights, mace, legalized guns,
        and there are plenty of folks

who get off on it.
    But not you, dear squirrel,
        to watch you is to see

the havoc of our days, how far
    we are from settling down
        (without medication),

so busy walling ourselves in,
    unable to distinguish the
        pitch of our happiness

from the depth of our despair—
as we wake to a world
we cannot see our place in.

These Fish

Unlike the depressed
   zoo panda whose fur and eyes
      have yellowed, these fish

are able to maintain
   such grace, against all odds,
      born in the wilds

and transported
   to the entry ways
      of Chinese restaurants,

hair salons,
   dermatologists' waiting rooms
      (below a poster of dangerous

moles). Like residents
   of new suburbias, they swim
      without old antagonisms

but for the occasional romp
   through artificial plant leaves
      or nip at a flashy tail.

Fertile as mice
   and equally discreet,
      you never see them

doing it, though something
   must account for their
      perpetual ease

and glow. Even when eating
   each other's remains, their mouths
      move slowly across the body

like a lover's, taking the flesh,
   making it theirs.
      Once, I stumbled upon

an unforgettable one
   living in exile
      on a secretary's desk

in a bowl no bigger
   than a cabbage.
      It was a gold fish,

undersexed and built
   like a jaguar. He could hardly move
      in the cramped space,

but he was still gorgeous,
   ebony eyes and well-endowed lips,
      his body the color of sunset

magnified in the curved glass.
   He shook his gills at me
      till the room spun around

and he was radiant.
   Radiant! Amphibious brute—
      that he could track me down

after all these years
   still offering nothing
      but desire?

TO MY THUMB

I could steer you into the cave of my mouth,
where only a few teeth and some words lived,

press you against my tongue, and you would fill
the emptiness of my first life, the first emptiness

I remember. You were the antennae that made it
work, the miracle that brought in all the stations.

Like a goldfish, I could hear everything
swim through the house, my thumb to God's ear,

the light backing off the carpet,
the skip in my mother's heart,

my father slipping on his mask. I could hear
the tide come in and fill our windows

with darkness. I would rock in my bed and
worry about my future. When I married,

would I wait till my husband
fell asleep to sneak you under the covers?

Or worse, would I have to tell him?
You were wise for your tender age,

how did you know my life would be a husband
and a secret, a comfort and a shame?

To An Old Sucker Fish

While the smaller fish take their perpetual lunch break,
nibbling and poking at leaves, or the slightest movement

in water current, grazing, roving clique-like from plant
to plant, bound to each other by the lowest common denominator,

you make yourself known to no one if you can help it,
sunk low in the water, your leopard skin camouflaged

along the bottom like a fallen tree or the shadow of a man
with his back turned. You don't even look like yourself,

the way your head rises to a puff pastry, then stretches
to almost your tail, more like a fish who has swallowed

the head of a man, or something equally hard to digest,
and then the eyes, tilted out like antennae, each held in place

with a rubber washer. When we brought you home in a vacuum sealed
plastic bag I could not look at you, repulsed by your abnormalities,

your lack of adornment, the way you insinuated yourself
into our new aquarium under the guise of algae eater,

offering round-the-clock custodial service. Back then
I decided you deserved your looks (we are what we eat)

and would make you the brunt of my jokes.
You were the only fish with an underside that could be measured

in cubic squares, the only one able to lie down
without being dead, though you scared me many times.

In the early days you roamed the tank walls freely
in broad daylight, I could sit with my face right up to

your flat belly and count the beats of your invisible heart,
which must be when I became mesmerized, drawn in by the soft,

pink opening pulsing on glass, as when one gazes long
into a lily, feels the force of its life. I think of all those

you have seen come and go, the pretty ones, admired for their
enthusiasm, how you prefer now to hide in the back

of the tank till all the lights are off. I wait in the pitch
dark to see you emerge, relaxed at last. Along your back

your own horizon unfolds in your dorsal fin as you
you propel yourself through deep water, like a sentence my heart

tries to make out, something that needs to be uttered
even if no living soul can begin to translate it.

Woman In Her Late Thirties

A woman in her right mind turns
to what's available, at age 37,
her daughter tattooed to her friends,
she hears the doors of motherhood
close, the windows, too soon,
leaving her alone inside her marriage vow
with a fistful of maternal instinct,
the way some men carry testosterone.

A woman in her late thirties knows
no way to stop herself, and will
take in any number of strays:
hamsters, fish, lizards, rabbits,
her insatiable heart running to Mr. Pet
at odd hours for supplies, till the house
is never empty, punctuated with small
black eyes, the rooms filled to varying
degrees of gestation, like water glasses
she can play with her spoon.

A woman in her late thirties wants
to get by without going to jail, her body
a wand she waves over herself. Early spring
she waits with her bucket for the great clatter
of frogs to appear on the pond,
the explosions of eggs that will soon follow.
Too eagerly, she rushes to pull off a glob
of the jelly mass for home, the dream of dozens
of tadpoles wiggling into view, like eighth notes,
all those hearts beating.

Woman With Hamster

The first part of the story
happens days before you
arrive on the scene with your freshly
converted aquarium. The mother
has eaten a few of her babies,
and your new pet has lived to tell
about it. No wonder he runs
the length of the cage when you
put in your hand. No wonder
he can't look you in the eye:
at ten days old, he's seen enough.
And now, no mother.
Or imagine this—every day
after your daughter leaves for school
you reach in the cage
to pick him up. You hold him
in front of your face, his ears
flared like bowling pins, and
speak to him in a sweet voice.
You know and the hamster knows,
your grip is too tight.
Your daughter, in fact, is the better
mother, the way she cares
for him and leaves him alone.
She has her life.
He's in your dreams, fast but memorable,
like an orgasm, or the cigarettes
you once loved. It's the fur
the color of smoke, the black eyes,
the way his nose deconstructs the air,
it's the way his heart pounds
in your hand. Hearts are addictive,
especially the small ones,
the kind you can actually feel
working their magic right up
against you, but who knows then
the psychologist will talk about that.
For now it's questions—
how much coffee and how many beers,

whether you exercise or have ever
contemplated driving your car
off the road. He writes it down.
Through the night, you hear the
hamster wheel throbbing,
relentless in its hold over you.

The Authors

CHEZIA THOMPSON Cager is a native of St. Louis, Missouri and a graduate of Washington University and Carnegie-Mellon University. She received the *Maryland State Arts Council Individual Artist Award in Poetry* in 1999 and 2001 and was Baltimore City's *Artscape 1996 Poetry Competition Award* winner, selected by Josephine Jacobsen for her chapbook *Power Objects*. Selected by Terry Blackhawk, as a finalist in the *Lotus Press-Naomi Long Madgett Poetry Contest* in 2002, she was also an associate artist under Ishmael Reed at *The Atlantic Center for the Arts* and a *Bread Loaf Writer's Conference* tuition grant recipient. In 2002, her work appears in anthologies including: *From Totems to Hip Hop, Catch The Fire, Dark Eros, Moving Beyond Boundaries-International Black Womens Writing Volume One* and *Thy Mother's Glass*. Recent journals publishing her work include: *Poet Lore, Bma: The Sonia Sanchez Literary Journal, Poetry New Zealand, The Baltimore Review, The Maryland Poetry Re-view, The Black Arts Quarterly,* and *Puerto del Sol*. Her first book *The Presence of Things Unseen: Giant Talk* is available through Maisonneuve Press. With co-producer Blair Ewing, Cager created the compact disk "The Road Less Taken: The 2001 Saint Valentine Sunday Poetry Marathon" as a notable, historical list of poets in the Mid-Atlantic region; also available through Maisonneuve Press or see www.spectrumofpoeticfire.com. Her *2000 Distinguished Black Marylanders Award* for her work as dramaturg or director in more than 25 productions, continues in Peter Lang Publishers special African American series with her "Teaching Jean Toomer's 1923 CANE," featuring photographs from the single full production of the 1923 Harlem Renaissance classic. A former arts reviewer for newspapers, she has published articles on poets/novelists/playwrights Earl Lovelace, Ntozake Shange, Wole Soyinka and other selected visual and performance artists. The A. Francis Sennar Film "Praise Song for Katherine Dunham" celebrates her life-long development as a poet in the language of dance. Her curator work includes exhibits: *Carl Clark: Photographer* (with co-curator Leslie King Hammond), *The Fine Arts Artists Market-Artscape 2000, Playing in the Dark Tower: Images From the Black Literary Landscape*, and special *Maryland Governor's Mansion Exhibits - Faces of the Real and the Imaginary, Power Objects* in the *Here and the Now, Landscapes of the Mind & Beyond*, and *Through the Fire – To the Limit: African American Artists in Maryland*.

CLARINDA HARRISS chairs the English Department at Towson University, where she teaches poetry and English-based prosody. She directs Brick-House Books, Inc., Maryland's oldest continuously publishing small press. Her books include *License Renewal for the Blind*, winner of the American Chapbook Award, *The Night Parrot, The Bone Tree*, and several scholarly/academic works; her latest collection, *Air Travel*, will come out 2004. Harriss' poems, essays and short fiction appear regularly in such venues as *Poetry, The Beloit Review, Prairie Schooner, Bitterroot, Genre, Epoch, Link* and many university quarterlies as well as selected electronic publications such as *Branches* (where an interactive version of "Air Travel" appears) and *Gloss*. Her poetry has won a number of awards, including the 2000 Milwaukee Irish-American Poetry Award and best-of-issue citations from *Poet & Critic* and other magazines. Her short fiction has won awards in several different *Story* Magazine competitions. Harriss has worked with prison writers for decades from the standpoints of writer, editor, and academic.

KENDRA KOPELKE is the author of two collections of poems, Eager Street (Stonevale Press), and Carpe Diem, Ants (Seedbed of Irony Press). She is an associate professor and director of the M.F.A. in Creative Writing & Publishing Arts at the University of Baltimore. She is also founder and co-editor of *Passager: A Journal of Remembrance and Discovery*, a national quarterly of fiction and poetry for new older writers. In 2001, *Baltimore Magazine* named her "Baltimore's Best Poet."

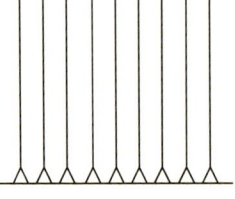